ORNAMENTAL CARPENTRY

ON NINETEENTH-CENTURY

AMERICAN HOUSES

ORNAMENTAL CARPENTRY

ON NINETEENTH-CENTURY
AMERICAN HOUSES

186 Photographs

BEN KARP

DOVER PUBLICATIONS, INC.
NEW YORK

Published in Canada by General Publishing Company, Ltd., 30 Lesmill Road, Don Mills, Toronto, Ontario.
Published in the United Kingdom by Constable and Company, Ltd., 10 Orange Street, London WC2H 7EG.

This Dover edition, first published in 1981, is a revised edition of the work originally published in 1966 by A. S. Barnes & Co., Inc., Cranbury, N.J., with the title *Wood Motifs in American Domestic Architecture/ "Phantasy in Wood."*
In the present edition, the selection and arrangement of the pictures has been altered, but the text remains unchanged, except that the List of Illustrations has been broken up to form captions.

International Standard Book Number: 0-486-24144-0
Library of Congress Catalog Card Number: 81-65710

Manufactured in the United States of America
Dover Publications, Inc.
180 Varick Street
New York; N.Y. 10014

PREFACE

The Age of Jackson saw the flowering of the sawn-ornament style in domestic architecture in America. So many newly prospering citizens wanted homes built that it was impossible for carpenters to indulge in the luxury of hand-chiseled ornament. Besides, these were houses for people of moderate means—mechanics, tradesmen, farmers—and the expense of carved or chiseled ornament would have brought the cost of the house above what such people could afford. Furthermore, the house carpenter was a man of the hammer and saw, and not of the chisel. If the exterior of the house was to be graced with ornament it would have to be something the carpenter could make with his saw and could hammer into a place with a few good nails.

It was the use of the saw as artist's tool that led to the growth of sawn ornament as architectural embellishment of the home. But if the American people had not liked this carpenter sculpture, this song of the saw would never have been sung. But the people did like it, and liked it well enough to keep it alive as a form of folk art right into the twentieth century. People liked it because its spirit was akin to the spirit of the day. Sawn ornament was like a banner hung out for a celebration, symbolizing confidence in the durability of opportunity in this land.

Lincoln, in a campaign speech in New Haven in 1860, said, "We wish to allow the humblest man an equal chance to get rich with anybody else. I want every man to have a chance in which he can better his condition." Ralph Waldo Emerson, in his famous address to the Cambridge chapter of the Phi Beta Kappa Society in 1837, declared, "Another sign of the times is the new importance given to the single person." Thoreau wrote, in *Walden*, "I desire that there be as many different persons in the world as possible; but I would have each one be very careful to pursue his own way and not his father's and his mother's and his neighbor's instead." In the opening lines of the first edition of *Leaves of Grass* in 1855 Walt Whitman sang:

One's-self I sing, a simple separate person
Yet utter the word Democratic, the word En-Masse.

It was in the spirit of Lincoln, Emerson, Thoreau and Whitman that the American carpenter wielded his saw. Brashly, on the facades of the dwellings of common people the carpenters found the way to sing of the individual.

Each house was built differently from its neighbor, each expressing the individual owner, yet all proclaiming the common faith in the American ideal of great expectations, faith in the possibility of improving one's lot. In a street of houses with sawn ornament there are rarely two alike. Yet out of this diversity a harmony resulted. "E Pluribus Unum" epitomizes the neighborhood of that time as well as the nation.

Our nineteenth-century arbiters of good taste deplored the uninhibited exuberance of the untutored carpenter artist and his "straining for effect." But this was the age of Davy Crockett, Paul Bunyan, Mike Fink and the other folk heroes, real and imaginary, whose fantastic feats and remarkable powers are still celebrated in song today. Sawn ornament is the expression of the same flamboyant spirit that created these legends. The boldness and courage of the frontier, the freedom from secular inhibitions, the self-confident venturesomeness that led millions of Americans into new places and new ways of living, worshipping, doing and making—all this is symbolized in the outpouring of sawn ornament from roof finial to porch apron. This was an art of the people, for the people, and by the people, celebrating the unfolding of the latent power of the new nation.

The photographs in this book, taken in various parts of the United States, deal exclusively with the sawn-wood ornamentation found on the exteriors of houses dating from the 1820s to 1910. Furthermore, the sawn ornamentation included in these photographs was purely saw-made—that is, no plane or chisel was used to bevel the edge of the ornament. All the ornamentation dealt with here is rectangular in cross section. Where turned work, done on the lathe, does appear in these photographs, it is a more or less unwelcome intruder, which the exigencies of photography could not avoid.

A section of this book is devoted to the shaped, cut or, as it is sometimes called, dimension shingle. This embellishment idiom of the nineteenth-century house in America is a historical and geographical concomitant of the other varieties of sawn ornamentation. The cut shingle is made with the saw and is rectangular in cross section, which are sufficent conditions to establish its kinship to the other forms of sawn ornament dealt with here.

Although photography can fib as beautifully as its sister arts, like its sisters it makes that fib appear as though it were the truth. No other medium could have made it so apparent that sawn ornament is an art of sculpture—indeed, sawn sculpture. The camera is also the ideal means for capturing that endlessly varied play of light and dark that sawn ornament brings to the nineteenth-century American house. The particular character of the American development of the sawn idiom owes a great deal to the qualities of American illumination, with its characteristic brilliance and variability.

B. K.

ACKNOWLEDGMENTS

To A. E. Woolley, photo journalist and author, for invaluable help with every aspect of the book.

To Alan DuBois, for help with photographic processes.

To The Research Foundation of the State University of New York, for several grants which made parts of this book possible.

To the owners of the houses, for permission to photograph their homes, and for their friendliness and help in supplying information.

To my wife Vivian, for helping achieve order out of a wealth of material and for coordinating text and photographs.

CONTENTS

I have seen thee, high and low,
Thirty years or more, and yet
'Twas a face I did not know;
Thou hast now, go where I may,
Fifty greetings in a day.

— William Wordsworth

ORNAMENTAL CARPENTRY
ON NINETEENTH-CENTURY
AMERICAN HOUSES

HOLES, SLITS AND SLOTS

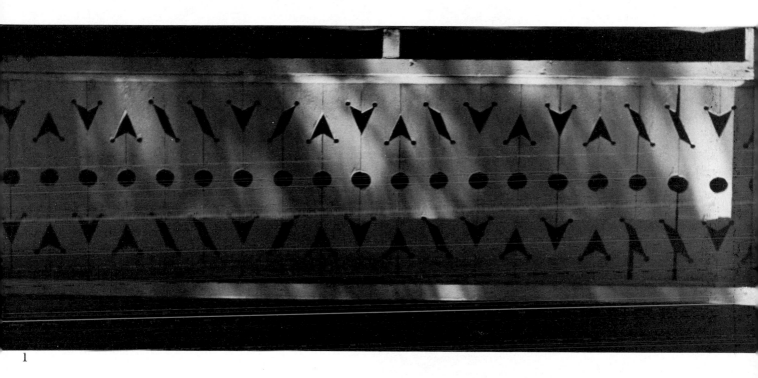

1

1. Porch railing, 1860's, Lacona, N.Y. Perhaps nowhere else in the whole range of sawn ornament does one feel so sharp a sense of being in the presence of a mysterious language as when one is confronted with the variety of sawn idiom which may be called "holes." These shaped holes, sawn in the wood board, have the presence of a strange calligraphy.

3

2

2. Porch railing, 1880's, Rosendale, N.Y. 3. Porch apron, 1876, Poughkeepsie, N.Y. One feels a religious quality in these signs. 4. Porch valance, 1878, Rhinebeck, N.Y. 5. Gable, 1899, Rifton, N.Y.

4

5

8

6. Vergeboard, 1880's, Kingston, N.Y. 7. Vergeboard, ca. 1890, Poughkeepsie, N.Y. One is aware that these symbols mean something. They did not have to be there. A vergeboard protects beam ends from the weather just as efficiently without these magic signs. One day, perhaps, an iconologist will decipher this writing. Meanwhile, as with other mysterious things, the mystery need be no hindrance to enjoyment. 8. Gable, ca. 1890, Ohioville, N.Y. As with other mysteries, we are permitted to classify them even though we may not understand them. We can even define, or make definitions of, what we do not understand. We may not be able to read the cipher of hole, slit and slot, but we can define these terms. A hole in the sawn-ornament idiom is a space surrounded by wood. Holes vary in shape. There are round holes, square holes, triangular holes, lobed holes, diamond-shaped holes, heart-shaped holes, club-shaped holes, spade-shaped holes, feather-shaped holes, leaf-shaped holes, flower-shaped holes, etc., as well as composite holes.

9

10

11

9. Gable, 1900, Tillson, N.Y. This is a language of hieratic ceremonial, such as man has used from time immemorial to consecrate his dwelling. 10. Gable, White Plains, N.Y. 11. Gable, 1899, Tillson, N.Y.

13

12. Porch post, 1850's, Port Ewen, N.Y. 13. Porch post bracket, Rhinebeck, N.Y.

16

14. Kingston, N.Y. 15. Porch railing, 1880's, Montgomery, N.Y. 16. Porch console, 1888, New Paltz, N.Y.

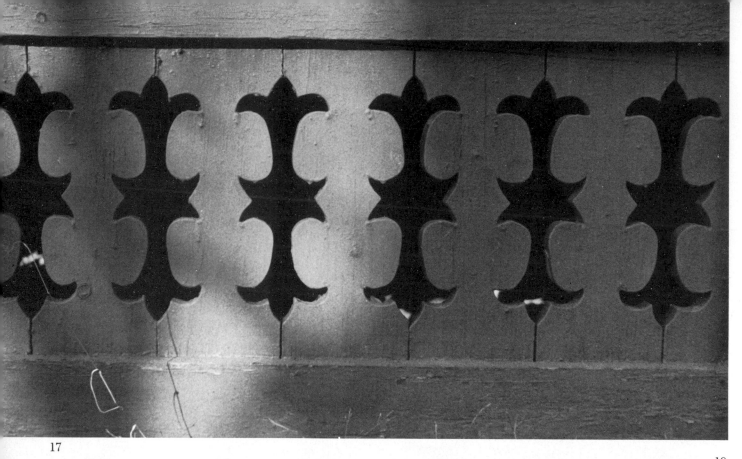

19

17. Porch apron, Poughkeepsie, N.Y. 18. Porch apron, Kingston, N.Y. A slit differs from a hole in that it need not be entirely surrounded by wood. On the other hand, it may be. The slit may be defined as a very narrow, long space. The edges of a slit may be no farther apart than the thickness of the saw blade that made it. A slot is a wider slit. Like the slit it may or may not be entirely surrounded by wood. The length of a slot is not so many times its width as in the case of the slit. Slits and slots are both predominantly straight, though not more so than holes are predominantly round. Bent or curved slits and slots have also been highly favored. 19. Porch apron, New Paltz, N.Y.

20

20. Porch post bracket, 1860's, Poughkeepsie, N.Y. 21. Gate, Cobleskill, N.Y. 22. Porch apron, 1880's, Kingston, N.Y.

21

22

23

23. Porch gable, 1880, Kingston, N.Y. 24. Porch post bracket, Oswego, N.Y. 25. Porch post bracket, 1880's, Kingston, N.Y.

24

25

26

26. Gable, 1880's, Gloucester, Mass. 27. Vergeboard, Saugerties, N.Y.

27

28. Porch valance, 1850's, Fort Edward, N.Y. 29. Porch valance, Colosse, N.Y. 30. Porch valance, Port Ewen, N.Y. 31. Porch apron, Poughkeepsie, N.Y.

32. Porch lintel pendant, 1874, New Paltz, N.Y. 33. Porch lintel pendant, Sloansville, N.Y.

34. Porch railing, Middletown, N.Y. 35. Gable, 1884, Marlboro, N.Y. 36. Barn door, Mahwah, N.J. 37. Porch post bracket, Palenville, N.Y.

36

37

40

38. Porch apron, 1870's, Poughkeepsie, N.Y. 39. Porch railing, Middletown, N.Y. 40. Porch apron, New London, Conn. Holes, slits and slots are immaterial — that is, they are space not substance. They are openings in the "closing" of surrounding board, passages through obstruction. Argus-like, they present a visage with a hundred eyes, all open. Dark areas surrounded by light, they are at the same time transparency amid opacity.

41

41. Porch post bracket, Quarryville, N.Y. 42. Gable, Highland, N.Y.

42

STICK DANCE

43

43. Gable, Clintondale, N.Y. The last spark of the ornamental fire of the nineteenth century was in the stick idiom. A decade after porch brackets were no longer used on new houses, the American carpenter wrote a brilliant chapter in the history of American architectural ornament with the elegant geometry of sticks that adorn the gables and porches of houses built in the last part of the nineteenth century and the first decade of the twentieth. The designs in this rectilinear idiom range from the simple use of two intersecting sticks to a rich orchestration of theme and variations.

44

44. Gable, New Paltz, N.Y. 45. Gable, 1895, New Paltz, N.Y. 46. Gable, New Paltz, N.Y.

47. Gable, Highland, N.Y. Since the sticks were all alike in these ornaments, the plastic variables could only be the length, arrangement and number of the sticks. 48. Gable, Highland, N.Y.

48

50

51

49. Gable, 1894, New Paltz, N.Y. The economy of means of the idiom stimulated the imaginative powers of the carpenters. One suspects, too, an element of Yankee thrift in the use of what otherwise would have been waste lumber. Every carpenter's workshop was strewn with odds and ends of lumber that could be trimmed down to make a usable stick, if a use could be found for it. It was in the temper of the times and the character of the American of those times to see the latent ornamental possibilities of combined sticks. With the lifting of the repressions of Puritanism, innate aesthetic feelings informed the eye of the carpenter. This capacity for sensing possibilities, which lies at the root of so much American material and spiritual inventiveness, was also operative in the carpenter of the day. 50 & 51. Gables, 1900, Highland, N.Y.

52

52 & 53. Gables, Middletown, N.Y. The shunning of exact repetition is evident in the stick idiom. It is rare to find two identical stick gable ornaments on a house. 54 & 55. Two details of a porch railing, Poughkeepsie, N.Y.

53

54

55

56

56. End valance of porch, Clintondale, N.Y. 57. Porch gable ornament, recessed, Highland, N.Y. 58. Porch valance, Newburgh, N.Y.

59 & 60. Segments of a porch railing, 1900, Highland, N.Y. Most engaging are the porch railings, where the carpenter invented startling asymmetrical compositions. Here the carpenter has developed a brilliant set of variations, revealing an innate sense of interval, rhythmic variety and spatial transposition. 61. Porch railing, 1895, Essex, Mass. There are twentieth-century abstract artists who would delight to find the plastic predilections of a later day in these designs, if they but noticed them. In this porch railing, on a house built about 1892 in Essex, Mass., the carpenter has not only abandoned symmetry, but has freed himself altogether from the constraints of verticals and horizontals to indulge in a powerful dance of diagonals.

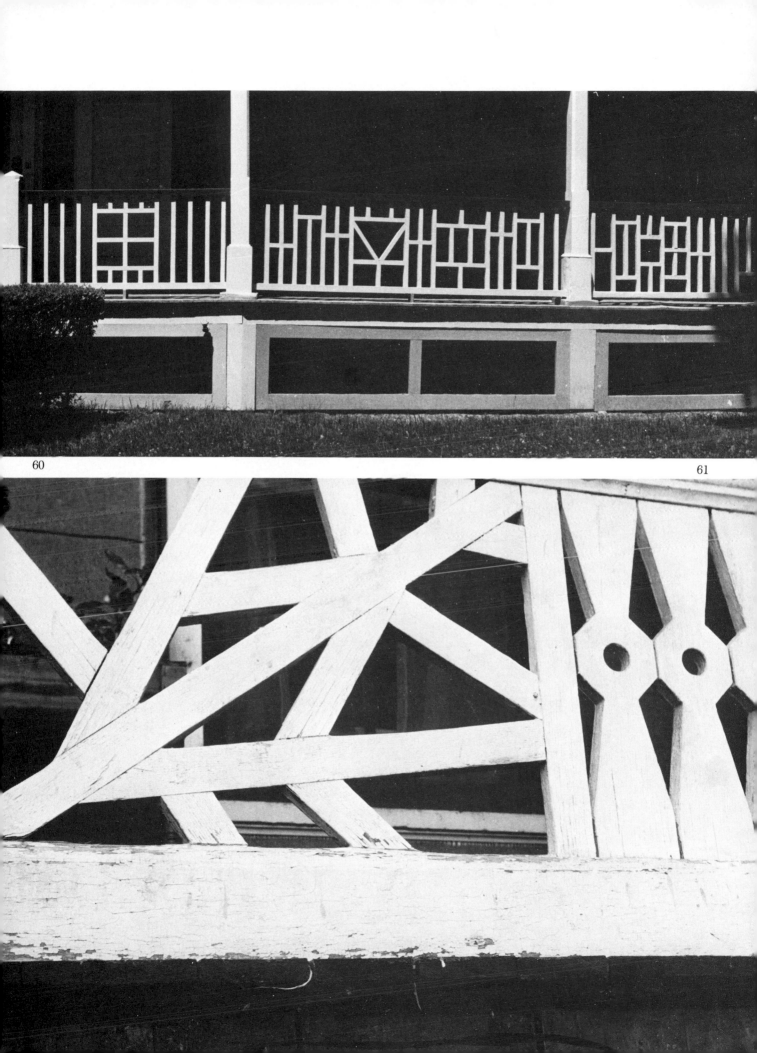

SCALES AND FEATHERS

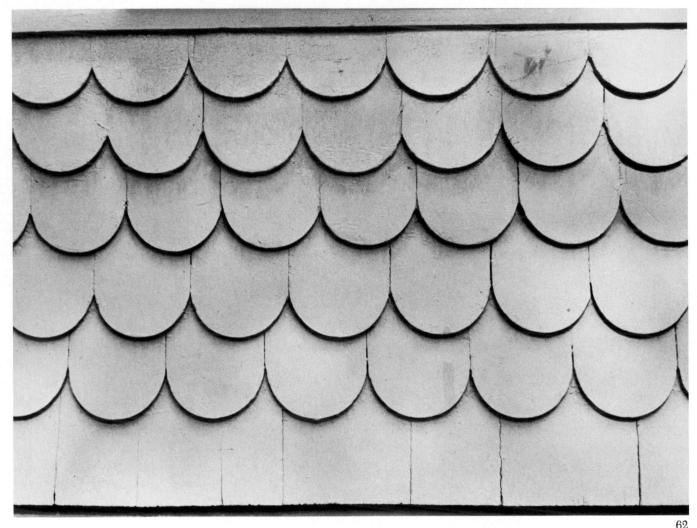

62. Frieze under window, Kingston, N.Y. 63. House exterior, San Diego, Calif. The varied shingle idiom is as much the sign of the Victorian era in America as the other varieties of sawn ornamentation found on nineteenth-century American houses. Quickly and conveniently split from logs of cedar or cypress, shingles afforded the early Dutch, Swedish and English settlers with an easier means to sheath a house than did the more laboriously sawn clapboard siding. But even in those hard-pressed times the instinct of embellishment asserted itself, as evidenced by seventeenth-century houses still standing on which round-cut shingles have been used in lieu of plain. The band saw, perfected after the Civil War, made it possible to turn out shingles of any desired shape with ease and speed. The carpenter used this resource to invent a fertile repertory of shingle shapes inspired by many sources. From playing cards came shingles in the form of hearts, clubs, spades and diamonds; the orchards inspired fruit forms, like the pear-shaped shingle; the kitchen garden yielded onion-shaped forms; the meadows were represented by clover and lily forms; the human form made its contribution in shapes suggested by various organs and parts of the body. The commonest variety, the round shingle, was derived from fish scales. When the exposed length of round shingle was increased, the form suggested plumage.

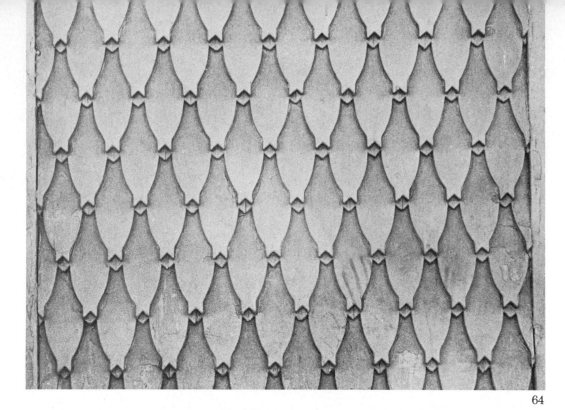

64

64. Spandrel, Oak Bluff, Martha's Vineyard, Mass. 65. Gable, Kingston, N.Y. 66. Porch, Buffalo, N.Y.

65

68

67. Bay, San Diego, Calif. 68. Gable and vergeboard, Buffalo, N.Y. Perhaps it is not accidental that the upsurge of inventiveness in the cut-shingle idiom coincided with the emergence of Impressionism in the 1870's. Both American carpenters and French painters sought to impart a rippling luminosity to their surfaces, and both found the same basic means to achieve their goal—namely, the fragmentation of the surface. The courses of cut shingle introduce into the treatment of the house exterior a vibrant, spotted play of light that is closely analogous to the Impressionist technique in painting, which aimed at the animation of the canvas to the highest pitch of liveliness. Both the carpenter and the painter were keenly sensitive to the enjoyment of the day's changing illumination as the sun moves across the sky, and as the cloud cover changes. Receiving the sun's rays at ever-varying angles, casting and receiving ever-changing shadows and reflections, the shingles present at one time of day a lighted face, at another a gleaming edge. Breaking up the wall surface into myriad lights, these house scales make the house kin to sparkling foliage and flashing water.

"I seek the varied stroke," Van Gogh wrote in a letter to his brother Théo in 1888. The Dutch painter had just turned to a new way of composing his pictures, character-ized by clearly defined areas, each formed by a repeated brushstroke of a particular size and shape. Contemporary American carpenters would have understood what Van Gogh was saying. For they too were seeking the compositional resources of an idiom of varied stroke, theirs in wood shingle cut with the saw. Both the Dutch painter and the American carpenter desired for their work the vitality and vivacity attainable from the energetic counterpoint of masses of varied stroke. Both relished the repertory of luminosities they could invent in this idiom.

69. Gable, Buffalo, N.Y. 70. Facade, 1890's, Deposit, N.Y. 71. Bay exterior, Falmouth, Mass.

72. Gable, Buffalo, N.Y. 73. Frieze, 1895, Poughkeepsie, N.Y. 74. Frieze under window, 1876, Kingston, N.Y. 75. Porch apron, Syracuse, N.Y.

74

75

76

76. Gable, 1888, Tillson, N.Y. 77. Gable and spandrel, Shaftsbury, Vt. 78. Facade,
New London, Conn.

81

79. Gable, Buffalo, N.Y. 80. Gable, 1860's, Syracuse, N.Y. 81. Facade, 1880's, Danbury, Conn.

83

82. Balcony, 1862, Philadelphia, Pa. 83. Upper story and porch apron, Poughkeepsie, N.Y. The cut-shingle idiom also played an architectonic role in the visual relationships of the masses that compose the house. By virtue of its characteristic tempo, a row or a series of rows of cut shingle constitute a more dynamic horizontal than clapboard. Thus, in the taller houses common after the Civil War, the rows of cut shingle were a means of reducing the new, unfamiliar verticality in the neighborhood. A cover of cut shingle next to walls of plain clapboard gave a bold emphasis to the bays, towers, balconies and other projections that characterized the post-Civil War house. On the other hand, continuous bands of cut shingle were used to bring such projections into a more contained relationship with the adjacent parts of the structure.

85

84. Bay, Kingston, N.Y. 85. Frieze, Bangor, Me. 86. Facades, Manchester, N.H.

86

87

89

87. Facade and bay, New London, Conn. 88. Gable, 1892, Port Ewen, N.Y. On occasion the carpenter shook off the mandate of horizontality to indulge his invention, or even caprice, in the disposition of his shingles. Here, a mysterious eddy in the stream of shingle courses, like soap bubbles pouring out of the window. 89. Facades, Sloatsburg, N.Y.

APPLIQUÉ

90

90. Under window, 1870's, Napanoch, N.Y. Between the three-dimensional freedom of the bracket and the surface vibration of cut shingle, the flat attached appliqué idiom plays an intermediate role of spatial bridge. In terms of light, the flat wood ornament—uniform in thickness, nailed onto a background—lies between the bracket, with its brilliant white surface against the dark of surrounding space, and the shimmering quality of cut shingle. It is both bold and gentle, having both the forcefulness of the bracket and the light touch of the shingle, both yin and yang. 91. Porch gable, Madison, Wis.

91

93

92. Porch post, 1858, Binghamton, N.Y. 93. Porch post, 1847, Kingston, N.Y.

96

94. Vergeboard, 1892, Poughkeepsie, N.Y. 95. Overdoor pediment, Ventura, Calif.
96. Overdoor and jamb, 1854, Sacramento, Calif. In appliqué work a greater delicacy
is attainable since the ornament is nailed to the background and does not require
structurally viable contact for support.

97. Entrance canopy console, Manchester, N.H.
98. Angle below cornice, Kingston, N.Y. 99. Entrance gable, San Diego, Calif. 100. Porch gable, Bennington, Vt.

97

101. Porch gable, Cicero, N.Y. 102. Porch gable, Oswego, N.Y. 103. Porch post bracket, Danbury, Conn. 104. Porch post capital, 1850's, Wawarsing, N.Y.

103

104

71

105

106

72

107

105. Porch gable, Oswego, N.Y. 106. Angle frieze, Sacramento, Calif. 107. Gablet over window, Charlottesville, Va. 108. Gable, 1860's, Poughkeepsie, N.Y. The appropriateness of the sun symbol for a rising country . . .

108

109. Lunette, Poughkeepsie, N.Y. 110. Gable ends and lunettes, 1860, Poughkeepsie, N.Y. 111. Gable, Poughkeepsie, N.Y. 112. Gable, Kingston, N.Y.

111

113. Porch apron, 1888, San Diego, Calif. Appliqué on porch apron of Stanford White house, San Diego, ca. 1895. 114. Porch post, 1850's, Rhinebeck, N.Y. A variation in this idiom is the use of appliqué in superimposition.

115. Gable, Kingston, N.Y. 116. Porch post capital, Fair Haven, Vt. It is in the appliqué idiom that a fundamental characteristic of sawn ornament—its flatness—is most clearly expressed. This is the result of the juxtaposition of the plane of the ornament and the parallel white of the background.

78

119

117. Frieze, New London, Conn. 118. Underwindow panels, 1890's, Bennington, Vt.
119. Porch valance, 1895, Kingston, N.Y. Great freedom of lateral movement is often
achieved. Appliqué permits an assemblage of noncontiguous units which appears to
float in the frame that surrounds it.

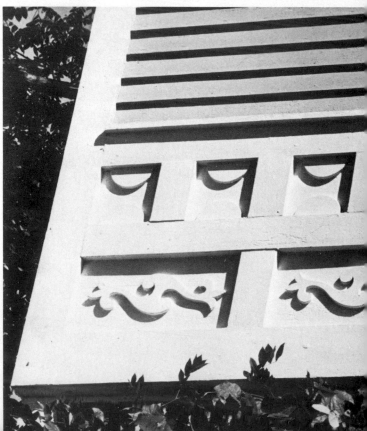

120. Porch valance, 1890's, Kingston, N.Y. 121. Frieze, 1897, Bennington, Vt. Jean Arp's appliquéd wood reliefs are the twentieth-century offspring of this older idiom. The Alsatian artist has made the plastic grace of this nineteenth-century idiom a part of this century's aesthetic sensibility.

121

BRACKETS

122   1

122. Porch post bracket, ca. 1850, Hurley, N.Y. 123. Porch post bracket, 1870, New Paltz, N.Y. The bracket is the oratory of the carpenter. Not that many a carpenter couldn't get up and deliver as good an extemporaneous stump speech as his fellow. This was the age that produced great orators and a great deal of oratory, and the gestures of the brackets are the gestures of the orators. The gamut of expression ranges from stately to frolicsome—varied gestures of a friendly, welcoming choreography. The bracket idiom may be thought of as taking its departure from a stick of lumber which begins, figuratively speaking, to get fancy notions as to how to vary the path it might take to get from vertical post to horizontal lintel. The bracket may be thought of as articulated log.

124

125

126

124. Porch post bracket, High Falls, N.Y. 125. Porch post bracket, 1838, New Paltz, N.Y. 126. Porch post bracket, 1850's, Rosendale, N.Y.

127. Porch post bracket, 1860's, Rhinebeck, N.Y. 128. Porch post bracket, New Paltz, N.Y. 129. Porch post brackets, 1850's, Rosendale, N.Y. The bracket is sculptural ornament in the round. It is meant to be seen from the porch looking outward as well as from the street. Nailed tenuously (but tenaciously), the brackets spring, leap, float, reach, dance, whirl and snake their way. Suspended in air, the bracket stands gleaming in the sunlight against the shade of the porch, in brilliant counterpoint to the bracket shadows cast on the wall. The shadow are warped versions of the bracket motif, changing in shape with the movement of the sun. The brackets are most beautiful when they stand in the failing light of the early evening, radiating light in the gathering dark of the porch and street.

129

131

130. Porch post bracket, Walden, N.Y. 131. Porch post bracket, Kingston, N.Y. The porch has been acclaimed as an American contribution to architecture. Without the porch the bracket idiom would never have had a chance to develop as it did in the nineteenth-century American dwelling. With the rich development of the bracket idiom the porch takes on a new aesthetic significance in the total composition of the house. The bracket is primarily an enrichment of the porch, but at the same time it makes the porch an entirely new entry to the house. The welcoming gestures of the brackets, their playful greeting, or their quiet presence like caryatids, make the porch a fresh experience.

134

132. Rosendale, N.Y. 133. Porch post bracket, 1850's, New Paltz, N.Y. 134. Porch post bracket, 1870's, Amenia, N.Y. 135. New Paltz, N.Y.

135

136. Roof brackets, 1870's, New Paltz, N.Y. 137. Roof brackets, Kingston, N.Y. The massing of the spatial rhythms of the brackets makes a special contribution. There is the play of interval between brackets, the counterpoint between porch and roof brackets, and the accentuation of the frontal plane in brackets used on the porch against the perpendicular movements of the roof brackets.

139

138. Porch post brackets, Kingston, N.Y. 139. Porch post bracket, Tarrytown, N.Y. The carpenter possessed the unteachable talent for creating an equilibrium of curves instinct with life.

142

140. Porch post brackets, Kaatsbaan, N.Y. 141. Porch post brackets, Bennington, Vt.
142. Porch post bracket, Kingston, N.Y.

SYMBOLISM

144

143. Entrance canopy console, 1880's, Poughkeepsie, N.Y. 144. Highland, N.Y. "We are all without redemption except we retain the sexual fibre of things — man, nude and abysmal, and indifferent to mere delicatesse." — Walt Whitman. "The symbolic values in a work of art may be unknown to the artist himself, and may even emphatically differ from what he consciously intends to express or from his conscious values." — Erwin Panofsky. "CHRISTIAN: The word of God saith that every imagination of the heart of man is only evil, and that continually. IGNORANCE: I will never believe that my heart is thus bad." — John Bunyan.

145. Porch end valance, 1885, Highland, N.Y. It is not always easy to decipher a given motif of sawn ornamentation. There are many disguises. In certain cases, however, the significance of the motif is not hard to find. As the French say, "Cela saute aux yeux." Or the English, "It's as plain as the nose on your face," the English being more to the point. It is not very difficult, for example, to decipher the meaning of the motif of the porch valance of the Abram Lent house. A series of long vertical slots arising from two contiguous circular holes, with another small round hole at a slight distance from the opposite end of each slot, lends itself fairly readily to interpretation as an abstract motif representing the male and female organs of generation.

146. Vergeboard, Smith Corners, N.Y. This vergeboard makes the probability of a correct reading of the motif in any other than a phallic sense so low as to warrant the statement that this is undeniably a representation of male genitalia. This degree of literalness of representation is at the naturalistic end of a scale of disguises ranging from complete abstraction to uninhibited naturalism.

146

148

147. Porch post bracket, 1860's, Falmouth, Mass. Franz Boas has pointed out that one of the commonest means of disguising a motif is to split the form and separate the parts, sometimes interposing another element between the separated pieces. In the house in Falmouth, Mass., by eliminating the porch post and bringing the two brackets together, the male genitalia motif becomes evident. 148. Vergeboard, 1867, High Falls, N.Y. The "icicle" motif on nineteenth-century vergeboards is so widespread as to be the one most likely to come to mind when the term vergeboard is mentioned. The term "icicle" is perhaps an unconscious avoidance of the recognition of the "verge" motif, verge being an old English word derived from the Latin *virga*, meaning penis. The true significance of the "icicle" motif is sometimes more apparent in the shadows it casts on the house.

149. Porch valance, 1880's, Kingston, N.Y. The American carpenter created many original variations of the ancient "eye" motif. This consists of a circular form lodged within a pointed oval or within a lozenge. It would be a monotonous laboring of the obvious to describe the manifold combinations of an enclosing form and an enclosed one, all symbolizing sexual union. 150. Gable and finial, 1882, Kingston, N.Y. The inventions of the American carpenter are often similar to, or exact replicas of, motifs and devices of past ages. One such is the ancient Maori symbol of sexual union which is found in this gable. 151. Porch railing, New Haven, Conn. In the porch rail of the house on Temple Street, the motif consists of horseshoe-like forms paired vertically back to back. This family of forms is of the most ancient lineage, including as one of its more recent developments the headdress of the Egyptian goddess Hathor. Hathor wears another symbol of femaleness, a set of cow horns. The horseshoe motif, like the set of horns, represents the vulva.

150

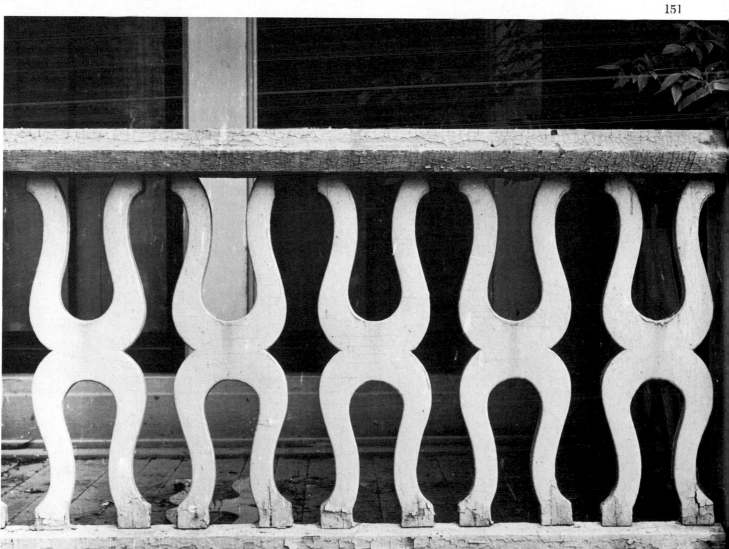

152. Porch post bracket, New London, Conn. 153. Vergeboard, Afton, N.Y. 154. Vergeboard, Buffalo, N.Y. The emphatic negative reaction of certain scholars and critics may be due to the unconscious recognition of the "ugly" subject matter. In referring to sawn ornamentation as "mysterious," Lewis Mumford perhaps recognized implicitly that it might have a meaning that eluded him. Understandably, the frustration of not being able to penetrate the mystery of sawn ornamentation might lead an art historian to consider it as issuing from an "abyss of ugly taste."

153

154

155

155. Porch railing, 1840's, Dobbs Ferry, N.Y. 156. Vergeboard, 1850's, Rhinebeck, N.Y.

159

157. Porch valance pendant, 1860's, Hyde Park, N.Y. 158. Gable bracket, 1872, Poughkeepsie, N.Y. 159. Gable, 1895, Poughkeepsie, N.Y. 160. Gable, ca. 1880, Kingston, N.Y. Overleaf: 161. Porch post, Cobleskill, N.Y. Porch post and railing decorated with breast-like forms. "All this effervescence is not for nothing; the friendlier, vaster, more vital modern spirit, hardly yet arrived at definite proportions, or to the knowledge of itself." — Walt Whitman.

160

161

FINIAL TO PORCH APRON

162. Gable, ca. 1900, Clintondale, N.Y. Sawn ornament is an art of out-of-doors, an outdoor sculpture intimately related to weather, to cloud cover, to sun and rain, and to the changing light of day from dawn to dusk. From the roof finial outlined against the sky to the porch apron resting on the earth, the idioms of sawn ornamentation are not only articulations of wood, but articulations of space and light as well. Let us recognize the wide range of expression in the work of the carpenter — the dignity, the humor, the delicacy and grace, the strength and energy embodied in countless compositions. Let us also recognize that the naïveté of the ornament is of the same vintage as the naïveté of the great American Experiment itself: "conceived in liberty and dedicated to the proposition that all men are created equal."

163. Vergeboards, 1895, Kerhonkson, N.Y. 164. Vergeboard, 1860's, Saugerties, N.Y.
165. Porch apron, ca. 1885, Fair Haven, Vt.

165

166. Porch valances, 1860's, Eagle Square, Vt. 167. Porch post bracket, ca. 1870, Scriba, N.Y.

166

118

169

168. Entrance canopy console, Falmouth, Mass. 169. Gable, 1890, Tillson, N.Y. 170. Porch lintel pendant, 1871, High Falls, N.Y.

168   170

171

171. Porch valance, 1860's, Hartford, Conn. 172. Vergeboard, Hudson Falls, N.Y.
173. Frieze over window, Buffalo, N.Y.

173

172

174

175

176

174. Porch railing, 1895, Essex, Mass. 175. Porch apron, New London, Conn.
176. Bennington, Vt.

177

178

179

177. Sacramento, Calif. 178. Porch railing, 1895, Essex, Mass. 179. Porch apron, 1898, New London, Conn. 180. Porch railing, 1890's, Manchester, N.H.

180

181

181. New London, Conn. 182. Porch apron, Poughkeepsie, N.Y. 183. Porch railing,
1880's, Hartford, Conn. 184. Porch apron, New London, Conn.

182

183

184

185. Porch valance, 1850's, Kingston, N.Y. 186. Roof finial, 1869, Binghamton, N.Y. "How can I but as here chanting, invite you for yourself to collect bouquets of the incomparable feuillage of these States?" — Walt Whitman.